POETRY now

The Promise Of A New Day

Edited by

Heather Killingray

First published in Great Britain in 2005 by
POETRY NOW
Remus House,
Coltsfoot Drive,
Peterborough, PE2 9JX
Telephone (01733) 898101
Fax (01733) 313524

SB ISBN 1 84602 004 2

FOREWORD

Although we are a nation of poets we are accused of not reading poetry, or buying poetry books. After many years of listening to the incessant gripes of poetry publishers, I can only assume that the books they publish, in general, are books that most people do not want to read.

Poetry should not be obscure, introverted, and as cryptic as a crossword puzzle: it is the poet's duty to reach out and embrace the world.

The world owes the poet nothing and we should not be expected to dig and delve into a rambling discourse searching for some inner meaning.

The reason we write poetry (and almost all of us do) is because we want to communicate: an ideal; an idea; or a specific feeling. Poetry is as essential in communication, as a letter; a radio; a telephone, and the main criterion for selecting the poems in this anthology is very simple: they communicate.

CONTENTS

WISE WARRIOR

In battle a tired ancient Brit,
Said, 'I fancy it's high time to quit
For I fear that the omens
Do favour the Romans -
So why be a stupid old twit?'

V B D'Wit

THE BALLAD OF DAVEY AND DICKIE

There was once a giant called Davey, he was over seven feet tall,
Bold and brave and virtuous, he was liked by one and all.
His best friend was a dwarf called Dickie, he looked to Davey
for protection.
If you wanted to be politically correct, you might say he was
challenged in a vertical direction.

They heard about a robber band and the evil they had done,
They tracked those robbers to their lair and slew them, every one.
The grateful local people rewarded Davey handsomely,
But a blow from a robber's sabre cut Dickie's leg off at the knee.

Then they heard about an ogre who had kidnapped a princess,
They fought and killed the ogre, rescued this lady from her distress.
She fell in love with Davey, he loved her with all his heart.
At the end of the fight, Dickie had one eye, when he'd had
two at the start.

They heard about a downtrodden land where a wicked tyrant reigned.
They started an invasion, that land its freedom gained.
That cruel despot they overthrew amid great jubilation,
But a palace guard attacked Dickie's left arm and performed
a neat amputation.

The grateful citizens of that land invited Davey to be their king.
He and his love began to reign amid joy and rejoicing.
They stood for truth and justice, righted wrongs and cured ills
And Dickie spent all his money on numerous doctors' bills.

Davey soon grew tired of this life of luxury,
He said, 'I'm off to seek more adventure, Dickie come along with me.'
Dickie leaned upon his crutches and glared with his one eye
And said, 'You'll go alone, I'll stay at home, so long,
farewell, goodbye!'

Said Davey, 'I never thought I'd hear you utter words like these,
Spurning valiant exploits for a life of slothful ease.'
Said Dickie, 'Between adventure and staying at home, I know
which one I'll choose. There really isn't much left of me
that I can afford to lose.'

If you seek a moral in this story I have told,
It's easy when you're big and strong, to be valiant, brave and bold.
To fight for truth and freedom, take the moral high ground,
be noble and pure.
When someone else will take the rap and get dropped in the manure.

B W Ford

DAVE - RESPECT

I feel to bear a tender loss
As life and death take one more turn,
I could see it in your eyes last time
You knew there would be no return,
With your illness biting hard
And all remediation spurned.

Who would have thought at Eastwood School
As we joined that infant class,
That our tracks would cross so much
In forty-seven years that passed,
From scruff-necks playing in Vic park
Through adult life so unabashed.

When we visited you last month
Nothing really much had changed,
We picked up where we'd left off,
Our easy going way remained,
No need to spar or fence about
With inhibition left unchained.

As I recall the memories
There's such a mixture in my mind,
Our weekend forays to the flicks,
A tanner for your chips to find,
Our scouting trips to Upwood glen
And rugby matches of both kinds.

We shared our early dating raids
With our girlfriends holding hands,
We holidayed in caravan
On Skegness beach and Dawlish sands,
Played tennis on the college court
Then chilli supper on command.

The qualities you brought to life
Amongst them many I recall:
A quiet sense of humour honed,
Your sporting prowess with a ball,
A simple no fuss attitude,
Reliability in all.

The message that you left with me
With quiet dignity instilled,
Was tomorrow may not come again
With opportunities to build,
So avoid all wasted chances missed
And strive to live a life fulfilled.

Malcolm Hulatt

THE PINK PARASOL

We all sat quiet and very still,
To hear the reading of the will.
The house was left to Uncle Jake,
Some shares in oil to cousin Kate.
A bee kept buzzing round my head,
When suddenly the lawyer said,
'And to my dear niece, Oriole
I leave my pink silk parasol.'
I gave a gasp of pure delight,
And clasped my hands together, tight.
Aunt May was tall with auburn hair,
Her parasol went everywhere,
It often clashed with what she wore,
That didn't worry her at all!
The parasol was edged with lace,
The handle had a fox's face.
Very soon the gift was mine,
That fox's face needed a shine!
I stroked the little silver nose,
There was a 'click' and then I froze.
My finger slipped into a space,
Then my heart began to race.
I felt something hard and round,
It was a ring that I had found,
Diamonds sparkled in the light,
Some rubies too, a lovely sight.
Attached to the ring, a little note,
This is what dear Aunt May wrote.
'To close the secret hiding place,
Press the eyes in the fox's face.
May these diamonds bring you love,
The parasol shade from above,
Be happy my dear Oriole,
Treat well, my pink silk parasol.

Diane Berthelot

Coral Reef

Coral reef is colourful and deadly.
Porcupine fish with quills to inflict.
Octopuses to squirt their ink,
then tentacles to constrict.

Sea snakes more deadly than man.
Poison extracted for antidotes when man can.

Lethal rays with sting so final.
Electric eels with volts,
make you feel electrifiable.

When in the depths of the ocean,
Get kitted out with snorkel, wet suit and a notion.

With oxygen and maybe a mix,
take a buddy in case you're in a fix.

Tanks full and gauges checked,
make sure your airway is not wrecked.

If in the depths you go where danger does lurk.
If you get the bends you will feel a burk.

Take care all you divers of the deep.
Me! I'd rather safari in a jeep.

Jacques Ellis-Knowles

THE BEGGAR

Sitting on the pavement as the crowds
passed through the mall
A shabby cap to catch his scanty gain,
With doleful eyes, his little canine pal,
With ragged coat to shield him from the rain.
The dog looked up. I tossed a coin,
and stroked his soft damp hair.
He licked my hand as if he knew,
Folks dashed by, but did they care?
If they did, well just a few.
The man looked ill, too old to beg.
Not fit to carry on,
And as I watched, I realised,
His breath and life was gone.
The dog crept over to his side,
And licked his face with love.
He didn't know that he had died,
Gone home to Heaven above . . .
I picked him up, his little paws
Were cold and wet with rain,
I softly whispered in his ear,
'You'll never beg again!'
The years have passed and we've grown old,
My little dog and I.
But love and kindness cannot hurt,
And won't, until we die.

Vera Pasonage

THE SINGING SHADE

Dog violets, intense yet shy
Grow in small clusters, shelter by
Protective boulders, moss-adorned,
In this green wood that seems newborn
With winter past. Sun stippled leaves
Make whispering roofs that interweave
To form a verdant canopy
Above star-pale anemone,
Sun's child, the lesser celandine;
While promise of June's eglantine
Fringes a small glade that discloses
A sudden joy of late primroses.
Now bluebells' mantle, balm for eyes,
Touches the heart with spring's surprise;
This, with first sprays of glimmering may
Deepen the spell of this rare day.
All grow where birdsong is relayed
Throughout the shimmering scented shade -
A parasol that brings delight
To hearing, feelings, touch and sight -
Its grace contained by treetops' height.

I gaze and questions asked eternally
Fade from my mind . . . It is enough to be.

Pamela Dixon

How Do I Look?

Would you tell me the truth,
If there stuck in my tooth,
Was something that just shouldn't be?
Or if right on my face,
Much to my sad disgrace,
A black smudge for the whole world to see?
What if there, on my clothes
Or on my pantyhose,
Was a tear of such terrible size?
Or if stuck to my shoe,
Was some terrible goo,
As I walked with my head held so high.

Would you stop me a while,
And just give me a smile,
And pretend that all things were okay?
Or just give me small chat,
All the while knowing that
This is how I would go through my day.
What if up in my hair,
Some strange thing resting there,
When I thought that my coif looked so well,
Would your mind say so pat,
'I look better than that!'
And decide that you never would tell!

I am never so sure
As I walk through my door,
And wonder that I should so fear.
That I am not judged
If my lipstick is smudged
And mascara is now in a smear.

My mind can just cope
With my fervent true hope,
That all things are the way they should be,
And that if on those days,
When my style's disarrayed,
It's the real me that everyone sees.

J A Brown

Some Day

Days of sorrow, days of joy
All come and go so quickly do they fly
The lucky have lots of good ones
The luckless struggle with the sorrow
Perhaps their day tomorrow
The day you think might be and face expectantly.
But no red letter, *God. Yesterday was better!*
You did have hope,
Days come and go to shape the week
And whatever it is you seek
The right day you will know
So live that day, enjoy full measure
Give or receive these days you will treasure
Some with memories clear, others to hold dear
With loved ones who are near.
Some days, best forgot but experience store
The future has an ever open door
Days by the score.
It's what life's worth living for
The happy days help cast out care and sorrow
Live on with hope, *new day tomorrow!*

Ron Powell

War Cries

War is so futile and it should be avoided
Ants to the slaughter, someone's son or daughter.

Our life, we are no longer in control
Politicians and propaganda decide our fate.
A press of a button, it could all be over
Mankind as we know it, gone forever.

Candida Lovell-Smith

Two Parts

Two parts make up one.
With one there are the lads,
the crack and those distant beers.

Two parts add up to me.
With the other there's all this,
I guess for now its home is here.

For one I'll be back,
I never really went away.
For the other I'm
still bleeding on that harsh freeway.

Anthony Welsh

TRAVEL IN TIME

When I was a child, we went to school
Down by the riverside,
We had to walk on our own two feet,
For no cycles had we to ride.

We used to sit down near the water,
When we had our dinner break,
And watch the boats as they floated by,
Trying to catch in our hands the waves

In those days there were very few cars,
We felt so safe as we walked along
Leaving that school by the riverside,
And making our way back home.

More than a mile we had to walk
Each and every day,
But with our friends had time to talk
As we happily went on our way.

Iris E Covell

OUR CROPS

There once was a crop so organic
It drove all its eaters quite manic
It never was sprayed
But made us afraid
And rushed the food pundits to panic.

Dudley Reeves

CARPE DIEM

When I retire, I used to say,
Even without sunshine I'll make hay.
I'll harvest wild oats I never sowed,
Make silage from grass I rarely mowed,
Go nutting in hazel woods that were,
Help endangered species keep their fur.

I'll rebuild bridges I tended to burn,
Inspire bored children, reluctant to learn.
I'll mend broken fences, especially vows,
Perfume the ambience of bitter rows.
I'll ban plans confused with platitudes,
Misinterpreted as beatitudes.

Now I've passed the statutory age,
When I'm presumed to be a sage,
Aspirations I once would hoard
Are worthless, seeming too long stored.
Stamina squandered in my youth
Intended to make me less uncouth,

Dissipates noblest of intentions,
Makes cynics of ingenuous inventions.
Don't lose your dignity, mentors exhorted,
But those were days when I cavorted.
While I appreciate sins of omission
I'm preoccupied with my next commission.

Challenges I'll never shirk,
My problem is - I can't stop work!

Malcolm Williams

STRANGER

I want to speak to you, Stranger
So I talk to you in my head.

I want to hear you, Stranger
Words you've never said.

I want to see you, Stranger
So I shut my eyes instead.

I want to smell your skin, Stranger
The scent by which I'm led.

I want to feel you, Stranger
So I touch myself in bed.

I want to taste you, Stranger
Till my appetite is fed.

Rara Avis

A Moment In Time

Give me a moment in time
A time to share
Give me a time in space

The love I give
Only years will tell
Give me a moment in time

The tenderness you give
Among the stars I see you
Give me a time in space

Years seem to come and go
The weather changes from rain to snow
Give me a moment in time

Time to care for you
Time to share
Give me time in space

Love for evermore
Treasured memories
Give me a moment in time
Give me time in space.

John Edney

TRUE BEAUTY

I saw the beauty in these eyes
Truer than the sunny skies
They gazed at me with love and peace
I thought, *will this wonder ever cease*
For this was beauty at its best
With eyes and smile and all the rest
But underneath this angelic cover
Is my true grandma and I love her

Tracey Burgon

ALLUSION

To be in a desert
And see a fountain of water
To be aged
And remember the energy of youth
To be unemployed
And imagine the earning of payment
To be weak
Then pursue nutrition to help bring strength
To be lonely
Yet envisage oneself surrounded by friends
To be shy
But have rare moments of being outgoing
To be disobedient
And on changing, receive reward
To be indifferent
Yet sometimes be overcome by enthusiasm
Surely these
Are dreams, hopes,
Wishes, desires
Which beckon
Calling for further fulfilment

C D Smith

Pregnant Pause

The last leaves brave the winter cold,
Steadfast they cling to the tree,
Clothing it thinly in amber and gold
Before the cruel wind sets them free.
Winter will have claimed its right to reign,
Trees will sway desolate and bare,
Frailty of limbs exposed for months
To the harshness of the numbing air.
At times they look so ugly and wizened,
Can they ever regain their splendour?
But, in the stillness of the winter's chill,
It's but a pregnant pause from November.

Buds are swelling beneath the bark
That covers each tapering spine,
The sap still flows to feed new life
Which will emerge when God gives the sign.
Then behold the glory of another spring,
Buds, blossom, leaflets so green
Clothing the dark, shivering, skeletal frames,
Trees the backdrop to set the spring scene.

Pat Heppel

You're The Mist And I'm The Tavern

You're the mist and I'm the tavern.
You're the mist in the midnight city, ubiquitiously dancing in the air.
I'm the tavern with doors opened.

You slipped in occasionally.
You made me moist.
You slipped out without saying goodbye.

The mist floated into another tavern in another city.
The tavern shut its doors and windows to keep moist inside, longing
For another damply misty night

Chichi Lai

This Night

As I fall into night
with you
lost in your arms
and the beautiful maze of your hair,
I pray for clouds and rain
to turn the sky dark
so that when the sun rises
we shall be unaware,
and even though night will have retreated into day
we shall only see darkness
and believe the light of day
to be far off.
And maybe,
maybe
this night shall last
forever.

Edward Lee

UNTITLED

The moon shines down
On his slowly beating heart
He kisses the eye of the storm
And floats ever upwards
Into unseen plains
And becomes one without meaning
One without soul

Oliver Trusler

Native Spring

Pattered and spattered, hither and thither,
Dripping with diamonds, dewy to wither,
Leafed without blowing and greener than grey,
Clotted and knotted, fainter than the day
Declining in the west, fade chromatic,
Rolling soft to tips, clinging like static,
Rain forth like rubies on countesses' skirts,
Plop into puddles and spew forth as dirt
And silence. Windows distant and darkness deep
Slam fast the shutters and fall fast asleep.

Thomas Clark

Mill Cottage, Milnathort

Mill Cottage stands just at the back
Of what was once a railroad track
Gone are the folk who once lived there
No more the smell of grain in the air.

In the yard the hens are nowhere to be seen,
And the grass in front doesn't seem so green
Some old stone steps, up to the wash house led
Well worn in the middle, with all the tread.

Beyond the wash house stood the old mill
And, but for fire might be standing still
Soldiers of the First World War were once housed there
And later, the Milnathort Agricultural shows and fair.

The names of Malcolm and Suttie, it is said
Were in ploughing well ahead
A straight furrow was what was wanted,
And man and horse were quite undaunted.

If more than a little nostalgic this may seem,
One is, I suppose, allowed to dream
Of days gone by, where I danced beneath the steeple
Of Milnathort and its kindly people.

Margaret Meek

TREASURE TROVE

Mum and Dad, war weary, slaved for their wage,
Cooped up in classroom and colliery cage.
Weekends were precious escape time to share,
Treasure trove of country walks, free fresh air.

City girl, country boy and clutch of three
Lancashire lasses, the eldest was me.
Slowest too, snail's pace, savouring the sights,
Treasure trove of hedgerows, deep felt delights.

Mum, Dad and sisters strode out ahead.
Now and then they'd stop and wait, 'nowt was said'.
Catching up, my pockets and heart bursting too,
Treasure trove of memories to last life through.

Now I'm a grandma, I still lag behind,
Husband and youngsters walk on, I don't mind.
One grandchild lingers and holds my hand tight,
Treasure trove of time to share pure delight.

Janet Bamber

Ode To A Footless Cadaver

I coveteth your footwear.
I desire the pair you sport.
I need them; how I need them,
Cos they're the ones you bought.

I love the pale blue canvas;
The logo on the side.
I want them. How I want them.
You wear them with such pride.

I asked you for them nicely.
I thought you would agree;
To give them. Oh please give them -
A gift, from you to me.

'Get stuffed!' you say in anger,
You are blind to my desire.
Refuse me; I still want them,
Will you not assuage my fire?

Hour after hour expressing
My dreams of footwear bliss.
Just know you're gonna lose them,
Also your feet, you're gonna miss.

I'm now beyond sane reason.
Those boots I must possess.
I'm off to find my hacksaw,
Just give up. Avoid the mess.

Barbara Paxman

ALPINE HOLIDAY

We're the Alpine Overlanders and off we stroll
Way up in those mountains in the Austrian Tyrol.
There's friendship a plenty and everyone's so kind,
A better bunch of people nowhere will you find.

Bob our driver is a very special man,
He gets you there as fast as he can.
We think he's worth an extra mention,
As nothing's too much for his attention.

On the way back from Innsbruck, Bob got lost,
But did we really care a toss -
We forgave him right away, as we'd had a lovely day,
So he took us back on the motorway.

Each night we have a 'pep talk' from our three musketeers,
Ron, Jim and Edward are our willing volunteers,
Who guide us up the mountain slopes,
When things get rough, they give us hope.

It's up and up, the going gets tough,
Still we don't mind a bit of rough.
It's well worthwhile for the lovely views,
Then it's down, down, down to have a snooze.

The hotel Brugger Sports is 'wunderbar'
People come from near and far.
The food's delicious and so nutritious,
No need to go to the local Spar!

It's cakes and coffee to sample their delights,
We've even had dancing on one of the nights.
A Tyrolean buffet with music from the zither,
It doesn't take much to make you quiver.

Our holiday's ended oh so quick, we can't believe it's over,
It's on the coach with driver Bob, we'll soon be back to Dover.
A lovely time was had by all, with memories to treasure,
Our many thanks to all concerned, who've given us so much pleasure.

Maureen Pendlebury

PICTURE

She stands in the corner,
back turned.
One small leg bent.
Her small head
resting on smaller hands:
She weeps gently.
Her blonde hair
falls to her shoulders,
how beautiful and frail she looks.
The dog stands at her back,
not on guard, as it would do,
but with a sadness on its face:
Head turned towards us,
beseeching, as if saying,
'This is a disgrace!'
Doll flung to the floor
to be played with no more.
All this do I see
from a picture,
A picture above my fireplace,
of a little girl, a dog and doll
and it brings out the sadness in me.

J Lanigan

Ill Fitting Genes

I hate these genes of such extremes
my sister is small and fair,
but I am big
and wear a wig,
that covers mousy hair.

I have these genes that must eat beans
but can't eat sticky pud,
I must exercise
not eat pies,
but lots of fruit is good.

I have these genes that can't wear jeans
I've fat around my hips,
around my thighs
by eating pies,
I use elastic but never zips.

I had these genes back in my teens
when I was tall and thin.
I lived on cake
and chocolate flake
and burgers weren't a sin.

I love my genes, I'll eat more greens
my parents are very old
eat what they like
never ridden a bike,
and like their wines, ice-cold.

Norma Davies

ALLOTMENTS

My husband has a garden
Down the road, away from here.
He spends a lot of time there,
And he wishes it were near.

He does a lot of digging
In the spring to start if off.
He's out in all that fresh air,
Yet he seldom gets a cough.

He grows a lot of produce
Root vegetables and greens.
Raspberries and strawberries
And different kinds of beans.

In June we have potatoes
Freshly dug and creamy white,
The skins fall off when washing them.
When boiled, they taste just right.

The raspberries are quite wonderful
Juicy and so big,
When he brings home a tray of them
I feel just like a pig . . .

Cos I can eat a dish of them
Without sugar, without cream,
There's plenty left to make desserts
It's like a glutton's dream.

He grows onions and small shallots
Cabbages and beet.
Peas and beans and marrows,
In rows so very neat.

The garden is a testament
Of all his love and care,
And when I cook the dinner
It's for both of us to share.

Elizabeth Stevens

UNMENDED FENCES

Unspoken words not said to loved ones.
Unsent letters full of regret,
Which shackle our souls.
Love tokens not exchanged.
Harsh words uttered which poison our brain.
Unmended fences; bridges not crossed.
Respect not regained, lie festering
So much pain in us remains,
Because we fail to say sorry.
Thinking there's always tomorrow,
Though in fact, few remain.
So in anguish we drive ourselves insane.
Animosity born out of inane trivialities.
Hardly arguments at all, that was plain.
So friends, we lose nothing by saying, 'Sorry!'
Offer someone a little praise,
Or a profound apology.
The failure to say a loving goodbye,
Can tear a wretched heart
And see us bereft, begin to cry.

Julia Pegg

LIBERATION

'Tis a sabbatical sentence hanging over the land
A sentence upheld by a seasonal command

The voice of damnation that comes to our shore
Whose whisper of winter turns into a roar

The weather is changing, the rain clouds obey
Turning the sky to a satanical grey

The inevitable omen breaching every defence
Keeping everyone prisoner in continuous suspense

The shadow of winter spreads its cold, endless night
Like a shroud of darkness stealing the light

Bringing the anger, the curse of the storm
And miserable colds that are ready to spawn

'Tis after the Christmas that people believe
Fostering hope for a conditional reprieve

The song of liberation does summon the wind
As the calendar turns to the prodigal spring

The warmth in the air does wallow in musk
Whose fragrance of spring does entertain trust

'Tis liberation from nature's seasonal machine
'Tis liberation from winter's dominant regime

David Bridgewater

On Paros And Naxos

There we were in a spit of sand
made ours by clothes and rucksacks;
in the scorching heat of island sun,
smouldering with the desires of life,
the ringing waves so near.
Amidst biting ouzo and tangy retsina,
alliances were forged in the heat,
by a sea so blue yet clear.

Some grew closer, some broke their links,
and all around lay bodies, like Hoplites
and Amazons, in battle fallen, stripped
down to naked flesh, exposed to glare
of sun or eye.

When sated by the heat, we ran into
Poseidon's cool embrace.
All was blue or yellow, no other colour yet.
In the fiery summer heat, the nearby tavernas
were a welcome relief, and the ice-cold beer,
fried squid and grilled snapper went down well.

We ourselves, were the meat in a yellow-blue
sandwich of sand, sea, sun and sky,
as the days and drachmas melted by.
As grains of sand, trickling through our toes,
the days ran out one by one,
so we turned our backs on our friend the sun.

But I'll never forget those Greek salad days,
in an ancient land of rock, sand and sea.
As the last embers of our holiday died,
when we still had youth on our side.

Charles Hurst

MEGAN AND CAITLIN

Two children on their way to church,
Both girls, and dressed in pristine white
They live their life in London Town
And celebrate this day of light.
Twins dressed for first communion,
They look so pretty for the day,
Out of their jeans and football shirts.
They look like angels, some might say.
Have the tomboys gone forever?
Where are their games and sibling fights?
Replaced by grace and perfect poise,
With tidy hair and grown-up tights?

What a shock for brother Liam.
Will he get his playmates back or
Will they stay like this for always?
Will the girls be fun, no more?
No, at the end their hair is messed.
Ribbons gone, they jump with joy.
They run around the grass like goats;

It seems they'd rather be a boy.

Laura P Williams

DECLINE OF THE SONGBIRD

I remember when I heard
Thrushes, starlings, wrens, blue tits,
Robins, finches and sparrows
Now we have the gulls
With their piercing cry
The heavy boys of the sky.

Beautiful songbirds
What have we done
Our stupidity is your peril
The injustices we have caused
Laying waste your feeding grounds

There is no time to spare
Children of the air
Sing your song out loud
So you will not be forgotten.

Kate Davies

HALLUCINATIONS ON THE TWELVE TO FOUR

Call it three inside the night or three before the day
when words or waves attack my ship and rattle sanity.

An army of eels
crawls across my skin like beads of sweat.

Strange is this complex light.
Only God separates surface from interior.

Colder now, ten degrees colder than that
when I hear the cry of a tethered goat.

Pressure's up. Pulse is down. Bleating's quite exquisite.
Nowhere to go, nowhere to hide, hyperventilating, fit to be tied,

when heavens crack and stench cloys the air.
The sea is a roiling, hissing predator, searching for prey.

Slipping and sliding through the midnight watch,
verbs clash and visuals do not match.

Something worrisome calls on me to jump,
to leap into the possibility.

Fortunately, sky is breaking and I pull back
to cast my nets and troll for bottom feeders.

Amused, grizzled by work,
I go below and squeeze into my bunk.

Meditating on three four of whisky's burning hell,
I eat a lobster squirming in its shell.
When I'm done I eat another one.

Ben Wilensky

AGREEMENT

Profound words heard in vain
War and peace it's just a game
As man explores outer space
The human race dies in disgrace.

Profits made, battles won
By another form of gun
What is yours, I'll have as well
Or I'll see you in Hell.

Handshakes in conference rooms
Agreements made already doomed.

Talk of trade and prosperity
Disarmament, you could have fooled me
Make a wish and make it clear
It's the last you'll ever hear.

B G Ryan

Spring

Lift your voices as you sing
Salutations to the spring.

Winter gone, come April days,
Glory of Heaven to blossoming sprays.

To passing winds surrender
their frail and dazzling splendour.

The sun of spring rides higher.
Trees catch the awakening fire

In the fold of leaf swelling
where birds will soon be dwelling.

Chaffinch, blackbird, robin, wren,
marking their territory again.

Flocks of gently crying sheep,
lambs run races keen to leap

For joy of being just alive.
And in the woods the violet thrives.

All makes the season a glorious thing
Summer's promise hidden in spring.

Idris Woodfield

FROM SONGS OF INNOCENCE

On a cloud I saw a child
And he laughingly said to me . . .

This cloud is very light
If Mum and Dad see me
They'll get a fright.

Reminds me of a fluffy pie
Floating high in the sky
My shoe has made a great big hole
Knocked it with the heel and sole.

Wonder how far can I drift
The world looks small
From my damaged lift.

Would you like to share my space
Perhaps we can ride to the pearly gates
Just for a visit not to stay
We can soon be on our way.

Do you think each angel has its own cloud
And gazes down on the human crowd
Maybe they even have a race
And then vanish without trace.

Yesterday I walked in the valley green
Just can't remember what happened in-between.

I think I've had enough
On this cloudy powder puff
Can you lift me down
Smile at me, no need to frown.

Gloria Hargreaves

My Youth

When came out of childhood, reached the age of 15
It seemed extremely risky
Always took care of my beauty
To flirt with any good-looking hunk, which was my full-time duty
But education was the first priority for me
Keeping in mind what is my goal in life to achieve
Kept my talents in sketching alive
I managed just wonderfully to survive
Gather with my cousins for a personal chat
Everyone's eyes on us three, being a rat
Sometimes I burst in laughter for no such reason
I dream of being the richest girl for season to season
I always feel pure, with freshness of being a youth
I did not waste it from being aloof
But it was a shame, some were extremely jealous of me,
Who I will name as a goof
Made a lot of good friends
Thinking it should never end.
I became more confident of achieving my goals one by one
In few months time I was in love
I have a slight arrogance
Definitely towards those with a mind that is narrow
I feel like flying in the air like a unicorn
Creating my own world as a lord
You too enjoy it, the time cannot be turned,
So take my words.

Farzana Nadeem

No!

Still I can't believe that he is gone.
We buried him and yet
I still expect
To hear his voice and see the smile
Gentle in his eyes
Connecting me to him
In recognition of enduring love.

He sat that day, at ease,
Graceful to the end,
And turned to me a face
Resigned and sad -
The last time that I knew him as he was;
But still I can't believe
I've lost the love I had.

Grey winter has passed
And springtime has returned
Yet I wait
For his warm hand on mine,
His kiss upon my brow.
My brain knows now
That he is gone
But still my heart cries, 'No!'

Valerie Sutton

YEARS

How have I come to be this old?
I should be gone. My tale is told.
But still relentless years advance,
Then dart away as if by chance,
Pretending that they have no power,
Nor interest in the date and hour
Of my demise. Heedless, headlong they race
Across the web of time and space.
Dispassionate, I watch the sprinters go
And wonder how it is that *days* go slow.

Louie Carr

Trial By Spin

David Kelly, scientist of note
Death precipitated by the self glory of others.
A fox with no escape from the hounds,
Cornered by bullies and the Bar.
Upstanding in unwarranted cross-examination
by men lacking in moral fibre
intellectually inferior,
relying only on platitudes and colloquialisms.
A victim of spin, super-egos, self-satisfaction and sadism.
Flailing, fragile, futile in the fray.
Family bereft of husband and father.
The hope is that the Grim Reaper goads the guilty into grievance
And that the innocent may rest in peace.

Gael Nash

A POLL 'O DJEE'

A statement of revoke, repetitively yielded,
Or merely a submission over reactions regretted yesterday.
True, some overuse reluctant repentance,
Yet sequential others reject, reacting . . . yearly!
'Sorry' oscillates, reflecting reality's yonder.

Aaron A Dunne

How Time Flies

The seasons come - the
seasons go
Sometimes fast, sometimes slow,
but this year seems it's in a race
I don't know how to keep the pace.
Yesterday went too soon,
Now it is tomorrow's noon.
Another week has just gone by -
My oh my, how time doth fly.
Life goes on its merry way,
Tomorrow is another day -
another day
another day

Dulcie Beatrice Gillman

THE GREY LADY

Uncanny grace the running boy revealed
As speed and flitting eyes of four years grown,
Scoured passengers for that which is concealed
And searching adult men are never shown.

His latent insight carried with his youth
No iron filing, but an arrow straight
Awaiting 'til his glance exposed the truth
And piercing, transfixed eyes struck Lady Grey.

Eye of beholder, suckling's silent voice
The woman dressed in yellow holds his look
But chances die in irony of choice
And age will take what knowledge always took.

And then the little girl among the crowd
Spies also her illusive, transient smile
And seeing through the multicoloured shroud
Of adults, will remember for a while.

She's sought by men and women just the same
Some spirit on a cliff repeating death
Some ancient saint, some adolescent flame,
All women wish to be, men to possess.

To lay this ghost and rest our minds we yearn
And watch each woman in each public place
But we shall never see her, for we've learned
To look too hard and miss that unknown face.

She lives in dreams, frustration, lost control
And all would wish she'd leave, as much as stay
To disconcert, crack confidence, tease souls,
That stranger, throne-usurper, Lady Grey.

Serena Shores

WRITERS

Plinking away, on a keyboard I type
Ignoring this smell that is so ripe,
My face looks so very sour,
What I could really use is a shower.
But I am on a roll, my character in heat,
I have a deadline that I must meet,
Sixty more pages and it will be done,
Being a writer is such fun.
I can write in my drawers if I like,
Taking a break to play with my tykes.
Don't have to commute to a job,
Just to my mailbox where there is seldom a mob.
Finishing off my intellectual gem,
I drop it in the mail to them,
Then I wait for the bucks to roll in,
Or the note suggesting
The best place for the manuscript is the trash bin.
Either way I am free to stay home,
Ne'er having to a job roam.
The kids and I have a wonderful time,
I just love this 'job' of mine.
Okay, this smell is getting to me,
Off to the shower, fifty-eight more pages
And I will be free.

Ferrell L 'Huck' Hickson

THE NEVER-ENDING STORY

Is it some kind of Gauguinesque riddle?
Where have we come from?
What are we?
Where are we going to?
The absurd answer
A long-lost race from outer space
God - a prehistoric spaceman.
Does the very same fate
Await this people again?
Is it merely an echo
Reverberating throughout the millennia?
A Heart of Darkness - like crushing prism of truth
Coming to all of us
Turning everything the Bible ever said
On its confused and dumbfounded head
Staring us starkly in the face
Once and ineluctably for all
Just like Conrad said,
'The horror, the horror.'

Hilary West

Morrow, Tomorrow

Ticking into the new year
Knitting minutes and seconds
With clip-click needles of time
Into a blanket of seasons.
Bubbling a marmalade stir
Of fortnights whizzed photo flash
Fast by holiday hoorays, as
The hip hop of spring sprung
Leaps into rain-riddled
Swimming pool summer.
Of vacations begun hooting traffic,
Car jam-jarred folk on
Weekend aways. Too soon
The red tears of autumn leaves
Cry down the face of
Wind-whispered, waning die tomorrow
Year. Massing in sweep-up jigsaws
Awaiting the benefit of smog-stifled
Snow. Mini avalanches of crystallised
Sugar look alike. Toll bell, wear black
Here comes gloved fingers. But enjoy
The finest flour of the indoor weevil's
Hello to winter woollies, cinder-scorched
Toes and welcomed writer's cramp.

Sarah Blackmore

GROWING OLD

'Over sixties', 'pensioners', 'the elderly', 'the aged' or infirm,
What it is to grow old, going bald or grey with a loo-brush perm.
Wearing winceyette nighties and bedsocks at night . . .
the dentures in a glass before you switch off the light.
We go off on our coach trips to the country or sea
Packed with sandwiches and flasks as happy as can be.
Just in case of a cough, pack Venos and Vic and . . .
a plastic bag and travelling pills in case we are sick.
Not to mention some brandy and smelling salts in case someone passes out,
Plasters for the bunions and corns, and the liniment for gout.
Wrapped up in our cardies and long johns to ensure we're all snug
With our potions for constipation or the dreaded 'tummy bug'.
We all fumble and drop things and talk to ourselves . . .
And put loo rolls in the fridge and sausages on the shelf!
We talk to the cat expecting an answer . . . oh, are you like me?
I sometimes think I'm going mad, I'm sure the cat would agree!
We are all getting shorter as we pile on the years,
So we keep taking our vitamins to remain 'youthful old dears'.
We have been there, and done that in the years gone by,
Don't worry, there's still life in us old dogs yet
Before we say, 'Goodbye!'

Margaret R Bevan

No Privacy Today (Psalm 139)

In this modern world with its computer system,
It seems that one's life will no longer be private,
Everyone everywhere, will be able to know what others are doing
all over the world,
Man seems to be getting beyond himself.

But for years now, I have said that God has had more than a world
computer,
In Psalm 139 He tells us He has known us before we were born,
He knows us from the womb, to the tomb,
In fact, He not only knows what is happening to us today,
But what will happen to us tomorrow, the day after and all
the tomorrows.

He does not need a man-made computer,
He is the Omnipotent, Almighty God,
Who created and made man in the first place,
And gave him the brains that are behind all modern inventions.

If it pleased Him, He could, in one flash of time
Displace the man He made and destroy the world.
But instead, He sent His only Son into the world,
Not to condemn the world and mankind of all their sin,
But to save them from the penalty of sin and death of the soul,
And to give them a new life, everlasting life with Him,
Yes with Him, in eternal bliss, where there is no more pain,
suffering and sickness,
But only if they repent of their sins and seek forgiveness at the Cross,
Where He was crucified for us all.

I wonder how many think of these things,
To live for today and all its pleasures,
Is what many seek after, but what of tomorrow?
Man does not know what tomorrow may bring,
Especially with all the accidents that happen today,
But I praise my God, I know Him, who holds tomorrow in the hollow
of His hand,
And am thus at peace, thank you Father, my Holy God.
Amen

Ruth Baker

Stirring Vicious Circles

The children I gave birth to,
The sons and daughters of Eve.
Whose prayers were unheard and so, unanswered.
Where did they get the pillars of strength they built?
I know not.

The truths I saved, sprinkled far and wide,
That was the platform I built for mankind.
Making a difference, trying to give peace a fairer chance.

The pillars of strength are beginning to crumble.
Hope is not flowing from the spring like it used to.
The community are putting up defences
The mantra has changed from all to for one.

The cross I bear from dawn to dusk,
As the villains become the heroes;
A conscience now is just a pest not a companion.

Hunting the weak,
Leaving the sick to die,
The actions speak louder than any words they say.

Grey and subdued,
Black and no warmth.
Bubbling under the strong currents;
Stirring vicious circles around and around and around . . .

Vincent Topp

Stop

I must stop to reflect again for this 'rat race' pace is not mine:
Oh give me time to refresh my soul and feast on things sublime!
I must stop to think again for many the pressures I face
through ear gate and eye gate and touch and smell
a pattern I need to trace!

I must stop to pray again, for people around me have need;
each carrying burdens too heavy to bear, because of others greed:
I must stop to write again, for fresh inspiration has come -
To push aside vision, thought, word and rhyme,
I must not now succumb!

I must stop to listen again, for voices are everywhere
Trying to influence word and deed - till inner peace seems rare!
I must stop to obey again the Heavenward pull on my soul
Yes, I must know the will of my God
For a world that's filled with woe!

Vera Smith

TODAY'S NEWS

Nothing much happened today.

A train crash near Bristol injured eleven:
The Queen has opened a new school in Devon:
A bishop said gays would not go to Heaven:
But nothing much happened today.

A tornado has ripped through a town in the States:
There was uproar in one of the Commons' debates:
The council is threatening to put up its rates:
But nothing much happened today.

Cars piled up in fog along the M4.
Scientists delving in far Ecuador
Discovered an insect not known before:
But nothing much happened today.

Jimmy and I are both keeping well;
Next door has got a new chiming doorbell;
Just down the road they've got kittens to sell;
So I thought I would snatch a few moments to tell
You all that's been happening today.

Marion Porter

MISPRINT

First time, I thought I'd got it wrong.
You see, the first line should have read,
March; in Africa another million die.
Instead, they wrote, *March: in Africa*
an other million die.

So I deleted 'space',
as if to say, 'to mass of millions
just add a million more;' to deny
they meant a second genocide;
ignoring bulk, purchased death
from different cull. The trick?

Sidetrack; cost out lost lives,
too cheap to hang on lines of print;
jetsam words of children starved, and
human flotsam sloshing shore to shore.

Starvation, sickness, slaughter speaks
with louder voice. I'd got it wrong,
I knew the first time line should read
March in Africa; an other million die.
It is the dying of a million other ones:
deleting space is the excuse, to hide
an other tribal cull, a different genocide
got out of hand; *March in Africa;*
an other million die: each one,
a misprint with will to live, their deaths
inscribed on woodpulped walls of print.

Alan Chesterfield

Bus Shelter

Bus shelters are much the same anywhere,
Metal framed, perspex sided, vandal worn,
Frequently with a side panel kicked out
And more often than not graffiti adorned.

I drove past one such the other day,
On a country road far away from home,
A road that ran through heathland full of dust
And ruined bunkers darkly basalt grey.

There a soldier stood waiting for a bus,
His gun propped up against the shelter's frame,
Golf club fashion, careless some might say,
While up the road tanks played out deadly games.

One battle practise zone with bus shelter
And bus shelters are much the same anywhere.

Margaret Hibbert

STRADIVARIUS IN SUFFOLK

Droning gently a sonorous cello
Follows the jig of the violin
While the pliant piano
Chimes a converging tune.
Beethoven galloping carrying
Borrowing the swaying trio.
Here, where I lived till I was four,
Here, where the schoolchildren
Leaning forward solemnly listen,
Here, where the green tiles
Catch and throw, sound and glisten
Fretting time is groomed and stilled.
The cello, sculpted long ago
By Stradivarius, is christened,
The Comte de Sauveuse
And has sung since the seventeen twenties.
How often has it throbbed
To Beethoven's pattern?
How often has it sung as it's singing now,
Booming along, gravely, gently,
Gravely, gently, without cease
Taking us all to a place of peace?

Gillian Bence-Jones

I Am A Bird

Yes, I am a bird
And I can do as I please
I can sit on rooftops
And rest in trees
It's my airport -
Free flights for fleas!

I fly in a pair
I'd never lose her
. . . I wouldn't dare!

Yes, I am a bird
I can soar high
And swoop low
Touching the sky!
It's a good job
Cos I don't like DIY!

Yes, I am a bird
A loveable thing
I quack now and again
My song I sing
I stick my head in the water
My feet in the air
(hunting for grub)
Cos I don't care!

I like to fly
But when I don't - I waddle
I wonder why?

What bird am I?
A duck of course
You must have guessed I'm not a horse!

T A Saunders

NOSTALGIA

On my bookcase by my wall
Many stories I have read
Like the adventures of 'The Famous Five'
Before I went to bed.

Another shelf and yet more books
Stacked neatly in a row
Are all 'The Little Noddy Books'
Which I collected long ago.

Noddy, Tessie Bear and Big Ears
Bumpy Dog and Tubby Bear
Mr Plod the policeman
In Toy Town - you'll find them there.

Another set of adventure books
Meetings held in the garden shed
Were where the 'Secret Seven' met
'Lollipops' was the password said.

'Enid Blyton' wrote them all
Easy to read and understand
The sets of all my children's books
Will always be at hand.

Trish Wright

THE STONES CRY OUT

The stones cry out of glory past,
These Gorsedd stones, where sun is cast
On this bright day of clear blue sky,
The stones themselves must give a sigh
And ponder, 'Will such glory last?'

The sea so still in Fishguard Bay,
This bright and glorious sunny day,
Not a ripple can be seen
In sea of blue, 'gainst grass of green,
But will such beauty ever stay?

As I look down on Lower Town,
A village now of much renown,
I wonder, 'Will it always be?
This old-world hamlet by the sea,
Or will one day its charm just drown?'

The stones cry out, though carved by man,
'We have been here since time began,'
Yet I must trust in God alone,
For He's my rock, my cornerstone,
Who holds all time within His hand.

For what of time did Jesus say?
'Heaven and Earth shall pass away,
yet my words must ever stand.'
In Heaven above and in this land
'A thousand years are but a day . . . '

Irene Hart

NEEDLEWORK

Lonely Miss Smith had a tapestry on the go
Her neighbours found her a right old sew and sew
She would sit by her window, cold and draughty
And lose herself in needlework, very crafty
With needle and thread, thumb capped with a thimble
Her elderly fingers were still very nimble
Her steely-grey hair, wrapped up in a bun
Glistening silver streaks in the afternoon sun
Her hands all crinkled, her face all wrinkled
And doing her favourite hobby, her brown eyes twinkled
Be it a tapestry or a pretty cross-stitch
She would revel in the colours, pallid and rich
She sometimes found the canvas very tricky
And with untidy threads she became very picky
There was nothing that she couldn't embroider
But what had made everyone avoid her?
She was picky and crafty and known to wheedle
An old sew and sew, who loved to needle.

Paul Spender

COMMON FEELING

When our cat Martha died
She my last link with Dad.
The day before
She kissed a scraggy, ratty,
Her successor Plato,
Black furred,
Number One on the block
Graced our home.
Then another scraggy,
Tiger shell Ibsen,
At first wild
Leaped around the kitchen,
Later so quiet, gentle insistent.

One hundred, old Queen's birthday,
Puppy going to be drowned,
So we had Queenie
Made two stray cats and a dog.

Fury of pain
My life devastated
A cripple.

Ibsen languishing
Taken to the vet
Did not come back.
Ten days hence
A terrible storm
Plato went.

Why did my cats go now?
Or did Father Tom in his trial lose Blossom?

What shall I do?
I liked the philosophies
Of Plato and the Doll's House?
The ideas, the intuitions.
Queenie misses the
Warm cat fur by the fire.

Drink Campari soda,
At my feet Queenie still rests,
Looks up at me with reproach,
While I think of God
And common feeling.

Paul Faulkner

An Old Rocker's Dreams

This old rocker thought he was Elvis
He rocked and rolled, swaying his pelvis
He dyed his hair black
Looking an old rockin' prat
All shook up like an ageing king Elvis.

This old rocker said, '*I still pull the birds*
Performing all those rock 'n' roll words'
But the notes he sang higher
Lost those great balls of fire
While strumming those old rock 'n' chords.

His body squeezes into the tight denim jeans
He still has his rock 'n' roll dreams
Sex, drugs and rock 'n' roll
Two out of three ain't bad I'm told
The third he can still dream it seems.

The blue suede shoes are nearly worn out
He's got a job to twist and shout
He's looking somewhat paler
He now needs an inhaler
He's not sure he should shake it, all about.

Rock 'n' roll will live forever
The old rocker's memories we can't sever
It is a great shame
Trading his guitar for a Zimmer frame
Don't cry in the chapel . . . the King lives forever.

John Babey

THE MEANING

A sense of numbness, whispers of dread
Like a lifeless ocean, circle my head
Creeping daylight sinking the sky
A single teardrop trickles my eye

Fragmented memories shrivel away
Floating reflections slow decay
My receding lifeline, light fades to sleep
No memories of joy or sadness to speak

A sensation of rising, stimulated, unafraid
Echoes of weeping begin to fade
Stillness and silence, transcendence, delight
Meaning of life? . . . No longer a fight

Colours unknown, I look without pain
Through dreamless sleep, searching in vain
As the shadow of an angel bows as he turns
Alas, the voice of Robert Burns.

R S Wayne Hughes

MEDALLIST

If there was an awards night for words
I'd award a medal to the word 'medallist'

'medallist' can equally apply to *the maker*
ie the one who *spawned* the medal
or to *the taker of the medal*
ie the one who's *worn* the medal
(and might, later, sadly, *pawn* the medal).

When I was young I foamed for golden fame
and a stout bottle-top attached to my lapel
was merely a rehearsal, or, clearly, so I thought.
If only I'd known that *making* that medal
made me, *technically*, a medallist
I'd have relaxed more, soft-pedalled
through the years, not taken life by the ears
for presenting me just *one* measly medal -
swimming, bronze survival.

Philip Burton

THE CROW

Bookish looker, dead mouse grabber,
the dawn crow calls down the Irish peat bogs.

Trencher-man of the wheely bins,
pioneer of old banana skins, calling,
'Ma,' singing against the pigeons.
But, she is not his mother.

Scarer of dogs, with his chisel beak.
The cat's sparring partner.
She tips the crumbs, from the bread bin,
over him.

The crow half scurries, half flies, away,
dejected.

David M Garnett

PETERS MARLAND

The rooks are not at rest,
And tell their neighbour so.
The valleys fill with mist,
And bat and blundering beetle
Hem the night about
Till all the lanes are darker still,
Where we had feared to tread
Yet I am glad we came.

For here it was, that night,
I first saw you entire.
Not the body the glass gave back,
The hollow and the shade,
But the person you.
And knew you had regrets,
And fears, with some small hope,
And held as much of love
As one can bear.

Knowing this I understand
Why deep set are the ways.
Why the best comes unexplained,
The scene surprise
With generosity.
And when that full sun comes
Together we will go
And unafraid ascend the lanes
The rooks at peace, and so are we.

Malcolm Currie

FRILLS AND FURBELOWS

How lovely you look
But there's pain in your eye
The pictures they took
Your feelings they belie
Through all time
Just a fleeting glimpse
Purpose-built for climbing
To the glittering prizes inch by inch
And when it's all over
People don't realise, as you
The memories you can cover
That are personal too
The drop of mascara
The covering of foundation
Sunk in wrinkles well earned
As life takes a turn
You'll have lots of anecdotes to burn.

Barbara Rumsey

WINTER MORNING

City
Muffled in dense grey fog.
Trees, roofs and chimney pots
Appear and disappear
In swirls of cold, wet clouds.

Birds perch,
Huddled on bare branches;
Cats curl
By hissing gas heaters;
Dogs crouch
Inside fusty kennels.

The sun,
A glaring circle, glows,
Pierces this thickening cloud,
Frees low city bridges
And calm river waters.

People
Walking across park lawns,
Now patterned with shadows,
Pass by painted benches
Still wet with misty drops.

Audrey J Roberts

SWEET BEAU

Oh how I love thee
Who brings sweet love to me

He who is all, so fine and fair
Dearest darling, passions where

Sweetest kisses cry.
Catching only soft maiden's sigh

Captivated heart divine
In love's embrace, we'll entwine

Vow my angel, words of love
Eternal whispers from above

Climax passions, Shangri-La
Lover's dreams on distant star

Surround love harboured well
Rejoice, oh unions, sweetest dell

Mountains high, valleys low
Oh my love, my sweetest beau

Dearest man's handsome face
Darling man's tender grace

Take your sweetheart's hand
Softly touch promised land

In your eyes I see the sky
As in your arms here I lie

Passions hold on so tight
Scarlet desires shine so bright

Comforting pleasure is only you
You take my soul, take me through

Fairy lands, so romantic, so free
Enchanting man, how I love thee

Ann Hathaway

WE MUST DISABLE THE AL-QAEDA

Their regime is unthinkable -
Extremists and fanatics twist
Their Muslim creed, to deal in war
Rather than peace. They will ignore
The moral limits that exist

In Western minds. A suicide
Bomber who slaughters innocents
Should be expelled from paradise.
Nobody in Heaven used vice
Foul as bin Laden's miscreance.

Frequently, Russians will invade
Neighbouring countries. Let's allow
Them to visit Afghanistan
And search out that Osama man
They're top spies. They'll make it, somehow.

Gillian C Fisher

FUNERAL

Somebody died today.
Anyone hopeful around.
Everyone had this to say,
'Alright mate. How's it going?', 'Sound'.

You wouldn't think,
That somebody died today,
We were in the pink,
At least it was going that way.

Somebody dies every day,
I am dying!
It is not word play,
I am not lying.

I can actually feel,
That I am on the way out,
But death has a strange appeal,
Yeah, death has a lot of clout.

Cut off the speaking flood,
The death of a pseudo-poet,
And pictures of me in the nude,
Will be circulated, I know it.

Fergus Hilton

OUR DAILY PRAYER

Lord, You came to give us life,
To set us free:
Our high priest,
Who opened up the way to God.
How can we not worship You,
Our holy God,
Who gave us liberty?
Faithful to us all life through,
Even though we falter
So many times along the way,
God, whose abundant love
Is so immense, so strong,
That we as mortals have
No idea of its depth,
Our daily prayer is to serve You,
No matter what age we are.
For You see us, Lord,
As You made us, and by
Our faith we will dwell with You,
Claiming Your blessing.

Bunty Hardman

My Bedtime Prayer

I ask the Lord to keep me loving.
I ask the Lord to keep me caring.
I ask the Lord to keep me leading.
I ask the Lord to keep me cheerful.
I ask the Lord to help me listen.
I ask the Lord to help me learn.
I ask the Lord to help me understand.
I ask the Lord to keep me well.
I ask the Lord to keep me growing.
I ask the Lord to bless my children and keep them safe.
I ask the Lord to protect nature.
I ask the Lord to strengthen the weak.
I ask the Lord to look after the homeless.
I ask the Lord that one day war will bring world peace.
May God bless everyone and everything.

Marina Smith

FISH NATION

They live above it and we live below it,
Water that is - and don't we just know it.
We've been hunted and caught since the dawn of man,
By nets and barbs - in fact, any way they can.

We come in schools and shoals, in pairs and alone,
The waters of the world are what we call home.
Some of us in saltwater - some of us in fresh,
No one's different, just like all the rest.

We're in the seas, oceans, the rivers, ponds and streams.
Life in the coral reefs is the stuff of dreams.
Our multicoloured cousins are resident there,
The danger's the same, but the climate is fair.
As relaxing as it is, they must always be aware
Of other undersea residents - be sure to take care.

It's the cod I feel sorry for, they get it in the neck.
Fished almost to extinction, and it ain't over yet.
They're trying to protect them, to let them recover,
Too late for some who've become a fish supper.
We're fried, pickled, boiled, steamed and smoked.
The whole damn thing's got beyond a joke.
Not content with all that, they pollute our space,
Every imaginable horror - courtesy the human race.

If you're not free to roam, but captive in some home,
Not vulnerable to attack, unless they have a cat,
You'll always be fed and be safe in your bed.
This may all seem very nice, but it comes at a price -
Like nowhere to go, and you're permanently on show.
Home is a bowl, or better still a tank,
Banged up with the others, what a cruel prank.

They've got us in aquariums - solariums and zoos as well,
Is there anything I've overlooked? I can't really tell.
One thing I'm sure of is I'm staying where I am,
Aware of the dangers of others, and of man.
Where I am will do nicely - at least I'm free,
Did I forget to mention my home's the Baltic Sea?

Fred Brett

DRAGON'S BATTLE

Troubled times
Destiny calls
And all around
His empire falls.

Down below
War is waged
Dragon roars
At battles raged.

The time arrives
The dragon flies
To the valley
Where brave men die.

Wings of shadow
Block the light
His enemies tremble,
In Dragon's sight.

His breath is fury
No mercy sounds
Death to those
Who claim his ground.

With destiny delivered,
He takes to flight.
A land is free
By Dragon's might.

M M Graham

FAILING ME

When I walk around my house
It's empty
My family are failing me
What about our country?
All I see is creativity
The uncertain and the unbeliever
Can I deal with change?
Are all the people deranged?
When I walk around my house
It's empty.

J Evans

Just Today

I got no time for worrying
got no time for hurrying.
Reet Petite,
bitter-sweet
can't seem to concentrate.
Fields gone, new road dug,
see the diggers, chug, chug, chug.
Hear her call, nature's pain,
feel the tears, watch in vain.
We should atone for what we've done,
how will we breathe when the trees are gone.
Boss is in, no 'Good morning,'
his face no smile adorning.
Just moaning and foaming at the mouth,
gritting and spitting, north and south.
The news is the same countrywide,
business is bad and misery beside.
I don't hate the man, he makes no sense,
but my dislike of him gets so intense.
Another lorry, another van,
another car, another man.
Tattooed, angry out the window he raves,
accuses and bemuses *me* about my driving ways.
This road is long, can't get along,
can't carry on.
Have to stop, pull in awhile,
start to smile.
Nearly home, job's been done,
kids are there, can carry on.
Pull in, home at last, head down, in bed I lay,
for tomorrow is another day.

Rick Oak

SEPTEMBER 2001

In remembrance we do the bizarre
Every early September I fill my house with flowers
More flowers than I can afford - roses - carnations.
Carnations were our dad's favourite - he was a gardener -
A lover of flowers.

I do it in dependence - in remembrance
On 7th September 2001 - I attended Manchester Cathedral
A conference on Anglican Spirituality
We 'do it' in dependence - in remembrance.

My dad lost his battle that day
Died of cancer - it consumed his body
Left him one strong arm - one strong hand
To grasp the heel of Baby Murray's foot.

I have no TV
Had no TV for fifteen years
At my brother's on September 11th 2001 - our house
The house where I was born, Roger was born.

Waiting for Percy Garner's funeral
Our dad Quarter Master Sergeant of the Eighth Army
Monte Casino 1944 - I gasped in horror - couldn't believe the load
Adding - adding to my heavy heart.

Couldn't believe my eyes - couldn't believe my ears
Load on load on load - pacing the floor - scuffing up the dog's
hairs on the carpet.
Percy's dog - black dog's hairs in scrumpled piles on the
pink, pink carpet
It once was our mum's pink carpet.

We did it
In remembrance,
In dependence,
Do it

Irene Clare Garner

'Twas Me

My misspent youth remembered well,
Breezes, trees, autumn swell.
Years passed by on wings of speed.
Quiet of solitude, a rare spent deed and attitude.
Family life, none could break the bonds,
Cemented there; loving careful fronds
Of parents, ceaseless, tiring, plodding on unending,
Wisdom's pearls forever rendering.
From eye to lips, twix cup was slips
Flesh grew old and passed away, died . . .
Four and twenty years died too, one old, one new.
I grew on, nothing stopped, changed or was slow.
Solitude evaded, escaped my grasp
To gates of openings for other paths, I longed to know
''Twas me. 'Twas me,' whispered low.
Love, love an imprisonment sealing forever more.
Then when freedom opens up the door
Once again recuperate from the broken chains,
Then it's dimmer, future a hazy view
Brain's patterns no longer new.
Solitude, I craved, stole quietly like the grave.
Touched the edge, entered, met halfway,
The beacon of life here all around this day.
In lighter shades a sunlight found,
A path that leads to sky from ground,
''Twas me. 'Twas me,' came the sound.
Here with beauty trailing, blooming, strongly light's prevailing
The full capacity, sounds and sights of memory
Joined together, past temperamental toils
A new world of paths trodden ere unfurls.
Of those passed before, on through this open door -
All was separate, yet combined
Of the young and old entwined.
No difference seen of the melancholy dream
Weaving a creative carpet of red.
Come forth those whose feet may tread . . .

The dead keep secrets, shrouded in rosy hues,
For one such like, who must know, and pay the dues.
Of the past, present, futuristic views . . .
''Twas me. 'Twas me,' faded away.

Norah Rawlinson

Magic At Midnight

I woke with a start and got out of bed,
then I heard the church bells peal.
I drew back the drapes - 'twas a gloomy night
the scene I saw looked unreal.
My garden was full of creatures galore
their eyes aglow in the dark.
Even the deer had come o'er this way,
they usually kept to the park.
Just to my left, where the woodland began
I saw there were dancing flames.
A massive bonfire was well alight,
the witches were at their games.
Quickly I dressed and left my room
as silently as I could.
I crept down the stairs and opened the door
then dashed to the edge of the wood.
I dropped to my knees and hid in the bush
to keep myself out of sight.
Suddenly everyone hushed and stood still,
a wizard came into the light.
The 'coven' immediately sunk to their knees,
some looked as if they might fall.
Then he raised his arms and spat out some words
as he towered over all.
He shouted one word and they all went mad
then all got up from their knees.
Like demons they started to sway and chant,
a sound like thousands of bees.
The wizard abruptly vanished from sight
as sudden as he had begun.
Order returned and the chanting ceased
now there was just a slight hum.
Some of the witches collected their brooms,
while others put out the fire.
Then all I could hear was a swishing sound
which faded as they flew higher.

I awoke to find I was snug in my bed
and dawn was just breaking through.
I really must stop watching 'Potter' films,
funny! It all seemed so true!

Elsie J Sharman

A Tasty Meal

'I am bored of this same food,' a frog said one day.
'I'm sick of eating worms and other types of prey.
I want something exciting, tasty and brand new . . .
something to tickle taste buds . . . egg and chips would do!'

He hopped along a garden and over a gate,
He landed in a kitchen right next to a plate.
'Go and wash your hands now!' he heard a mother shout,
'As it won't be too long before I dish this out!'

The frog hid behind the cold tap, away from view.
'Hmm . . . I wonder if I need to wash my hands too?'
Thought the little green frog who soon was thrilled to bits
When he saw what the mum was serving . . . egg and chips!

'Now's my chance,' thought frog as the mother left the room,
With one leap he cleared the taps, a sink and a broom!
He edged a bit closer and reached onto the plate,
In a flash some chips had gone, in fact he'd eaten eight!

Suddenly he saw that the mother had come back
So he tried to jump for cover to hide the fact
That a frog had eaten all the food on the plate,
But his tummy was so big, he couldn't lift the weight!

'Come here you little rascal!' he heard Mother shout.
The frog let out a burp then managed to jump out . . .
Into the garden and he hid under the bin.
He rubbed his big tummy. 'Phew!' he said with a grin!

Adele Whittaker

My Big Bed

I've just had my first grown-up bed,
I'm not a baby now my mum and dad have said.
It's upstairs in my bedroom, looking big and bold,
I can always sleep in my mummy's bed if I get too cold.
My teddy's on the pillow, waiting for tonight,
He can keep me company until it gets light.
It's time to go to bed now and kiss my mum goodnight,
Blankets all around me, cosy and tight.
But I'm sure I heard a movement underneath my bed,
Monsters live under there, I'm sure I've heard it said.
But I'm far too scared to take a look and see if it's true.
My teddy's looking at me, is he frightened too?
So I lie awake in my new bed, and try not to make a sound,
I can still hear movements, it's the monsters moving round.
I really am frightened now and jump up out of bed,
I think I'm still a baby, I'll sleep with Mum and Dad instead.

Catherine Lambert

ECHOING

It's like a dripping from a tap this
pain, crisp, relentless, echoing.
It bounces off the hardened enamel of what I try to be,
staining it the bloody colour
of iron.

A stain I think only I can see
and try to ignore.
A stain that I can't wash out.

I feel like a white shirt on a sunny day,
marred under the bright glow.
My stain so obvious under the light
that I fear to stay and fear to run
because there is nowhere
to run to.

And this stain stares at me
like I shouldn't really have it,
that it's not mine,
but it is.
And the more I scrub,
the more I wash,
the more it stays.

And red
is such a beautiful colour.

David Gatward

GRASSHOPPER GRAVEYARD

Down where the deadly holy lie,
grasshopper heaven rocked on by,
going to the rhythm of the jungle-
grass beat,
grasshoppers raspin' in the heat;
Oh how they partied every day,
dancin' on the dead where they lay,
grasshopper graveyard is where
they come,
when Mardi Gras season has begun;
So if you listen really well,
you will hear it like I tell,
hoppin' and a-jumpin' in their play,
the Mardi Gras beat
is the grasshopper way.

Amanda Kitching

A Friend

A man is fortunate and wealthy indeed
If he has a friend when he is in need.
When the going is good, when times are bad
When happiness abounds, when occasions are sad.

When the sun shines, when furious tempests blow
When prospects are bright, when troubles flow
In all times, wet or dry, whatever the end
beside you will always be a true friend.

Look around, contemplate with hand on heart
Can you tell fair-weather friends or true friends apart?
Which is which, in ascertaining, where do you start?
The test of time, a strong occasion will produce the right heart.

A true friend is created through trust, love, respect and care
Can you respond with more if you dare.
You and your friend will have a bond to treasure
Each other's company will generate pleasure.

When you have a loved one or a friend so true
In most people's life they are too few
A friend is life's precious gift to you
Respect, love and care for them and they will return it
to you know who.

Terry Godwin

My Child

As I hold you in my arms
Rocking to and fro, it calms
As I place you to my breast
I have realised my quest
To make you strong, so you can be
The beginning of my eternity.

J R Griffin

They See You

Limitations may frustrate
many people with their fate
take criticism
in your stride
it can only help
your pride.
Don't blind yourself to the fact
that you're fine the
way you were made,
it's those that see you
as a 'thing' that need
their head examining.

Jade Bosworth

Who Knows?

We all know people in our time
Who say they need and love us,
They'll say we make their lives sublime,
And swear by stars above us,
Then along the way there comes a day
When they no longer heed us,
So, do they need because they love,
Or love because they need us?

Matthew L Burns

The Potion

The crippled old witch knocked on her door
And gave her a potion, the only one that she had,
She promised it would give her happiness forever more,
But there was one ingredient, before dusk that the girl must add.
The witch fled, before she could ask,
Leaving the bottle behind.
'What must I add to this flask?'
The question still playing on her mind.
The girl longed to be happy and rid of fear,
As she was a captive all alone,
The prison she was trapped in was all too near,
As it was the place she called home.
She hysterically tried whatever she could find,
To add to the potion before sundown,
She was quickly running out of time,
Her mind spinning around.
She looked out at the black night sky
And felt a tear roll down her cheek,
'That's where I wish my soul would fly,'
She whispered in a voice so weak.
Her tears were liquidised pain,
Her life was in slow motion,
As she cried the water fell like rain,
And her tears fell in the potion.
She soon realised that the spell was complete,
As a trace of emotion is all the mixture missed,
She was then set free and swept off her feet,
From then on, her life was bliss.

Rosanna Anstice

CAGE 399: RABBIT/WHITE

Drip,
Drip,
Drip.
They call me a guinea pig
Even though I'm not.
I'm a rabbit,
By default.
Not that you can tell
Now that I'm bald.
They shaved off all my fur
And applied chemicals
That burn.
They want to see if it stings
When it drips
On human skin,
So they pour it on me.
It goes on for weeks.
It goes on neat.
I wonder if they'll ever stop?
I wonder what I did wrong?
But still it . . .
Drips,
Drips,
Drips.

Rachel C Zaino

A Dog's Plea

I look up, with hopeful and pleading eyes,
I wag my tail, but inside my heart cries.
Please, look at me, don't pass me by.
I'm so alone and afraid, and I don't want to die.
I didn't do anything wrong, and I'm not bad,
But nobody loves me, that's why I'm so sad.
I wish you would take me home with you,
My shattered faith in humans to renew.
I know it's not your fault, you're not to blame,
But for thousands of dogs to die unloved, is a shame.
Please look within me, to my faithful heart,
In a body so bruised and torn apart.
Yet still I could learn to trust once more,
To be a happy dog, with a future in store.
Just give me your love, a warm bed and some food,
In return I will love you and always be good.
I'd be so content just to lie at your feet,
A better friend than me you could never meet.
So, if one day in a 'dogs' home' you see
A plain old dog, please hear my plea.
Don't pass him by without a second glance,
Don't walk away, please give him a chance.
He may not be pretty, or have a pedigree,
But that sad, plain old dog might just be me.

Maureen Roberts

Darling Namesake

I keep my pets in pots, my potted pets
They might be called. Their lovely blooms
And foliage delight: they decorate my rooms
With vibrancy and colour that offsets
The soulless scene of sofas, chairs and walls,
And every now and then they may present
The treasure of a heart-refreshing scent
That when combined with floral grace enthrals
The mind; but mistress of them all appears
In spring to greet the sun, perfection's queen,
The amaryllis, beautiful, serene,
Source of the darling namesake who endears
Herself to me as Ann-maryllis, lady fair,
With whom alone its glory can compare.

Frank Littlewood

THE POET AND THE CRITIC

Some critics say the poets
Are lost in mere fancy
Their art nothing but flux
Of lies and imagination.
Thus do some critics witter,
Twitter, rant and rave
Our false judge, jury
And emasculators.

Begone!
You sad, cruel creatures
Of abyss and night
Whose only motive
Is to capture our souls
And with slow, icy grip
Squeeze out all light.

Begone!
I roar once more,
Let our souls wander freely
Our senses delight at
And breathe in
The fresh life of day,
Let us live!
And above all,
Let us play!

Trevor De Luca

SPIRIT WITHIN

They live within a secret realm
These secret souls as they dance
Where is this place? you may ask
As they show their dancing shadows.

They show us their many colours
So bright, clear and clean
Rainbows shine within them
Like a bright, shimmering stream.

You watch them in awe
As they land upon a leaf green
Or flutter by like neon nymphs
To a bewildered eye that's seen.

Is this their dream they give us
Or ours within their realm?
This beauty we see dancing
Within their magic land.

R Mills

Hindus And Muslims

How much progress have we made?
From Stone Age to the computer maze
It's all worthless, it's all futile
When we fight for a piece of land
We extend no understanding
We give no helping hand
How is the partition in mending?
When there's no compromise, we take a stand
We hoard the memories of the past
What can we build our present on, alas!
When we talk about the past with hatred
We prejudice our children, we continue this charade
Are we really a religious nation?
Do we honestly follow the scriptures with passion?
So, why did we burn our brotherhood alive?
To the screams of help, why turn a blind eye?
Were both sides not human?
Couldn't humanity prevail?
Why is the inner god asleep?
If he is not within us, he never existed.

Naina Mehta

TEA FOR TWO

What an elegant sight meets the eye
For two weary, footsore ladies,
They have walked Oxford Street to The Ritz -
Which took them ages!
Their designer bags held by tired, aching limbs,
Faces aglow at the sight of the tables -
Let's splash out and have some Pimms!

The waiters are dressed just so,
The order is taken, they wait.
The decor is truly British,
With cucumber sandwiches on plates.
The cake stand sits proud amongst the splendour of the table,
Covered with damask pure and fine.
The teacups chink and the sugar lumps melt.
The pair relax, reflecting their lives,
That of secretary, mother and wife.

Barbara O'Leary

For Mum - Early Spring 2004

Entering, leaf-soft feet,
Here, site of your shrine
Where meeting is in still
Place of the heart
Closer now, in gentle way of nature.

Trees, gilded in early
Spring light, new joy in
Birdsong, here, place
Of closeness, we are
Calm, all is well.

'Special friend' dancing
In endless light-quiet
Music in eternity-joy
Has come in our morning, life
Is endless, love never dies.

George Coombs

THE DEAD GIRL

The dead girl had no secrets, her diary told no lies,
Unveiled between those pages, she told who she despised.
She showed no one any mercy, she didn't think they'd know,
These words were written for herself, and never would be shown.

A story of malice, of pain coming from all ends,
She wrote of thick betrayal, coming from once friends.
She screamed out on those pages, waiting to be free,
She told of how she cried, but no one seemed to see.

She wrote when she was dying, she didn't know what to do.
She wrote of how others said the same, no one had a clue.
To conclude she said she was sorry, that she just couldn't hold on,
She said she hoped no one would mourn her, when she was gone.

The writing grew dishevelled, tears stained the page,
She cut into the paper, blinded by her rage.
She wrote of all her weaknesses, why couldn't she give in?
She listed and apologised for every time she'd sinned.

She prepared to give up, so shared her tales of love.
She wrote how much she'd miss her friends when she went above.
She cried again and broke down, another attempt failed that night,
She was so fed up of trying, she just couldn't win this fight.

There was a final entry,
One simply saying she'd try,
That was the day that she gave in,
The day she chose to die.

Rehana Allison (14)

Making Music

Your fingers as light as butterfly wings
Caress and tease me until my heart sings
Your kisses make me surrender to you
And enjoy everything that you do
To my pulsating body that you play
Like a fine instrument every day
I just can't get enough of your sweet love
Thrust inside me and I coo like a dove
You fill my body and you blow my mind
You are a guy of the special kind
You know what I like and you do it well
And you like what I do too I can tell
We come together in a blaze of heat
When both our bodies and both our souls meet
I am your woman and you are my man
And we make music whenever we can.

Ann Blair

A Day To Remember

Remember always of the beauty and views
Images to treasure which you never lose
Ventures for all, old and the young
Imagination runs wild, everyone having fun
Nature in every house, castle to explore
Going home time, no, you want to stay more
Treats and teas at the old barn house door
Outstanding free day to stay outdoors or rest
New every time you visit the north-west.

P Brewer

Aries Reincarnate

A fine shepherd, so you are
Wesley Armstrong!
Your ewes are trim
their lambs are fat
the ram so well supplied.

Neat are your fields
as your sheep nibble
round the rushes
leaving small
green islands.

There's shelter too
under the hedges
to keep them dry
from Fermanagh's
regular rain.

I often think that
to be one of your
well-kept sheep
Wesley Armstrong
would be no bad thing!

So much so I am minded
to ask at Heaven's gate
to come back as one
of your Brockagh flock.
A ram perchance.

Paradise deferred
and in seventh heaven
butting and tupping
I'd be well looked after
So I would!

Anthony J Brady

Guilt Pays You Back In Another Way

(Dedicated to Faye Marsden)

It's only a matter of time now, Faye,
Yours not mine - as they all say,
Until finally you will pay
For what you did that day.
Now we all live with that in our own way,
You've even taken the girls away,
And their visits to talk and play,
But still you can't hide your guilt away.
All the innocent ones have suffered for what you've done,
While your guilt loads your head like a loaded gun.
As you struggle with your guilt each day,
Try as you may, it won't go away,
You'll always remain the guilty one.
But when he's gone and you've both had your fun,
Suddenly you'll feel like me, heartbroken and numb.

Only then will you know what it feels like
To be on the receiving end - to lose
Your lover, soulmate and best friend,
Something he never was in the beginning
And will never be, even in the end.

Then suddenly you'll remember that day, Faye,
And realise also the price I had to pay.
Because of your unfaithfulness that day,
I too had to live with that every single day,
And carry your shame in a different way.
Those memories still haunt me - how you
Punished me for my loyalty?

Graham Hare

STUDENTS, AFRICAN

Telling them that God was a construct
and that the real question was, *why?*
and the classroom glowing
with anger and pity
and me feeling alive.

Telling them about oppression
cloaked in evangelical mission
and early childhood sepias
of ringed female necks a foot long
and a *savage* with a bone through his nose.

And the one with
the Stars and Stripes headscarf
whose eyes had drowned
in my wine bar seduction
in deep indifference two nights ago
now telling us the bone
was a fashion statement

and suddenly leaving the room,
with me knowing
that on her mobile
it says, *I love you Jesus*
and Jesus loves me.

Ken Champion

GETTING OUT

The tone is of muck
in ruts British Rail brown
scattered gulls like T-cell-like
under a microscope

A sun with die back
one that once shone on everyone
competes with the Costa Del

one. The Pack fights in law, blood,
sherry at the ready
an ISBN for the decline
of its eccentricity

The first man walks out for a duck,
the pavilion where it was
in the beginning, is now and ever
more shall be, in every eventuality -
(light, rain, tea)

sentiment scent on a fair skininnings,
a draw the calculus of memory:
discrepancy of said and meant,

a sediment of tea leaves,
for the reading of meaning.
At worse, a pall of silence.
At best an edge
(think, thick, willow)

dream shoved under my
head. A lavender pillow.

Ann Marie Eldon

Progress At A Price

Woodland and hedgerow, coppice and brook.
Birds' habitats vanishing now.
Demolished by man in his endless quest.
For new roads, new houses, new towns.

Many a lark, a ground-dwelling bird,
Has lost her home for sure.
No more her song so sweetly sung,
Delivered on high in the air.

We seldom see the white throat,
The swallow or the swift,
They're all part of nature's store,
Our good Lord's precious gift.

Do we know the devastation
That progress often brings,
Have lost birds soared their way to Heaven,
Seeking home on heartbroken wing?

So take care of the birds that visit your garden,
Feed them, keep them strong,
Your reward will be great when summer arrives,
They will sing you their beautiful song.

Dorothy M Mitchell

A PRAYER FOR BEN

Dear Heavenly Spirit,
Ben tragically had to be put to sleep
April 27th 2004.
His pain is no more.
I miss him more every passing day
As I travel along life's way.
I pray, hear my prayer,
Keep Ben in your eternal loving care.
Dry the tears I weep,
One day at your feet,
Ben and I will meet.
Together we will travel the Golden Ridge
And cross Rainbow Bridge
To join the angels' band
Forever in Summerland.
Amen.

Elaine Hicklin

9/11 Enigma

Eleven's twin digits, symbolic of towers,
Micro-midgets, widgets with powers,
While effigy pins stick through great Satan,
Did friends of Bin's pick too the date on
Which to launch death's hours?

Was 9/11 (once thought attrition),
Conspiracy-driven upon its mission
Of sacrificial mass bloodbath,
Whilst leaving in its aftermath,
Some clues to fuse suspicion?

Insider stock-gains go 'unwatched'
By those who vet; as yet unscotched,
A pet goat story's import so special.
It rendered shattered towers non-crucial:
Some pilot merely botched.

A forecourt film of the Pentagon struck,
Was quickly whisked away by truck,
Its driver; in the FBI,
Just happened to be passing by,
What serendipitous luck?

Yet no such quick command was noted,
For NORAD cover; so honour-coated,
Three score and more call-outs they tallied
The year before; none dilly-dallied
Till 9/11 was floated.

Bin's clan plus loot; all flown away,
No questions put, but ours will stay,
Like: why should - for those killed galore -
A free memorial tower soar
Yet for their deaths - none pay?

Watcher

In The Wake Of The Echo

Perhaps the rubble has been finally rake-cleaned,
with it some finger, eye, nose or other,
which could not tell where it came from -
Anita's, Hugh's or Julia's . . .
every part of the twin-gods of this tower yet to spring anew,
shall haunt the brain in the flesh-plaster of its walls from
Anita, Hugh or Julia . . .

Yet the echo threatens with volcanoes of fury
whose meaning is a certain kernel of human tragedy
the arm of the monster is long and regenerative:
this courage to re-erect the monolith of fraud and deception
wears the wreaths of our essences
the crown of the twin-gods of fate is barbed and unsure;
it radiates in the blood of the massacre, in the killing of
the innocent; seek, as business goes on,
the ultimate tablet to assuage the gods of the earth,
whose rousing, slow and ghastly, may recrudesce
in the wake of the echo.

For no more shall we with rains as tears,
fond of flowers though we may be,
join another procession to the field of many flowers.

Chidi Amaechi

FIFTY YEARS OF ROCK 'N' ROLL SESTINA

Rock 'n' roll has lasted half a century it appears,
Since Elvis first invented it, it's lived through fifty years,
And in that time, its devotees have shifted many beers,
Its competition comes and goes, and passes through our ears,
But none of it will last as long as rock 'n' roll, my dears,
It just goes rockin' on and on, so put away your fears.

I gave my life to it without any fears,
It will last forever, or so it appears,
And each time you hear it, your feet tap, my dears,
I bet it is still here for fifty more years,
It will set our toes tapping, and ring in our ears,
While we're sipping our coffee, or quaffing our beers.

We used to drink pale ale, not iced lager beers,
And going home plastered was one of our fears,
Cos Mother would catch us a clump round the ears,
And working hungover's not all it appears,
We learned a few lessons thus, over the years,
But rock 'n' roll music would soothe us, my dears.

When we had red noses, like Santa's reindeers,
As a sign of p'raps having sunk too many beers,
We learned how to handle it over the years,
So a picture of sobriety's what appears,
Our rock 'n' roll music still regaled our ears,
Anaesthetised us against life's little fears.

As Elvis and Buddy songs rung in our ears,
We had everything that we wanted, my dears,
Our teddy-boy lifestyle is all it appears,
With music and dancing, and just a few beers,
Our macho appearance allayed any fears,
We seemed more grown-up than our young teenage years.

The fifties and sixties were our magic years,
With Radio Luxembourg plugged in our ears,
Of deafness in later life, we had no fears,
There was nothing to beat it, I'll tell you, my dears,
Washed down with a couple of nice ice-cold beers,
Our teenage contentment was as it appears.

Rock 'n' roll gave us satisfied ears, so it appears,
Fifty years, no fears, musical perfection, my dears,
It just took rock 'n' roll and a couple of beers!

Mick Nash

FRIENDS

Friends are those that are always near to you,
No matter where they are, they always get through.
Time of joy with you they share with feeling,
Even though to them they have no meaning.

Joys and sorrows shared together,
A good friend with you will be forever.
Life will have its ups and downs,
Lots of smiles and lots of frowns.

When it's time to have a party,
Good friends are welcome, not the nasty.
As we go through life a lot we meet,
From working class to those with seat.

No matter what class they come from,
You can make friends with everyone.
A group of us in a big family,
Had orders we were going overseas.

There we found it best in groups.
Otherwise you find yourself in the soup.
Bullets fly, from nowhere they come,
If you're in the road, it ain't any fun.

One day a big explosion came,
I was caught then and my end came.
But a friend was there to see me through,
That's why I can write this poem for you.

Ken Copley

Dignity

Diagnosed with depression, it's hard for me to accept this
You see goals I set in the past, achieved them for I'm a worker
The questions I ask now, was it that I didn't take a rest?
No break did I give myself, a breakdown was what slowed me down.

Now I'm run into the ground, no confidence can be found
Each time I try, a knock back every time
What happened to those goals? I can't even open a door
Determination to succeed is draining from me each day.

If only a kind employer would come along
Just providing for my children would fulfil my goals
Teaching them that working is better than a state living
Not adopting and inheriting a world of depression.

So come on all you employers, the challenge is set for you
Take on that disabled person, a wee chance is all we need
Let us prove our worth to you, for workers we are that freely
seek employment with you
We only want to earn our living, not drown in depression.

George Petrie

PYGMALION

It can only be you in this stone: white like priests,
your legs having just paused there
your body a road that waits for me to come.
I see you like a blind: with my fingers,
I hear you like a deaf: with my touch.
I hit the stone at its roots.

Light moves for you rising from under your toes,
pouring them through my fingers; I align your gazes,
make them painful, a thousand kisses into this one hit.
The blood of the marble already on your mouth.
I hit and hit at its veins.

Love is more tender underneath, I fall in love whilst
you rise to the surface like an underwater plant,
flatter silence, your touch heavy with my flesh.
I cannot stop now, my thoughts absorbed, becoming you.
This trail of white you leave behind; you have almost arrived.

It can only be you this stone: white like priests,
marble emptied of its heart. I spare the stone, hit the light.

Elena Tincu

UGLY BUDDY

Yes! You called me buddy, each time I visited you
You even called me buddy, when you visited my country too
You showed me films from Hollywood, Walt Disney's make-believe
The bright lights of Las Vegas, cards hidden up a sleeve.

But what you failed to tell me, those cards held hidden faces
Faces I couldn't recognise, your hand held all the aces,
You came to free my country, from Saddam's deadly hold
Those faces you had hidden, began slowly to unfold.

In terror I stand upon this box, naked for all to see
Electrodes attached to my genitals, a woman's smile ignores my plea
The pain from the beatings is awful, too much for one to bear
I'm told that if I move, my body will fry and sear.

Stripped of total dignity, degraded beyond belief
By these GI tormenting monsters, soon all will hear my grief
From so-called Christian perpetrators, with such wild imagination
Will this torment finally end, to complete Iraq's castration?

In your so-called civilised culture, what you've done seems
a little extreme
You've made me pay and suffer, for Saddam's evil regime
For all that you have given the world; you really haven't a fan
Around the globe you're known; as the ugly American.

Your downfall will be those snaps; your wartime souvenirs
Of forced unnatural behaviour; blindfolded, manacled, in tears,
How stupid are these Americans, bandying this evidence around?
Together with their female lechers; their minds must be unsound.

Do they think that if they plead; they were acting from above?
That this will excuse their debauchery; 'pull the other one, my love,'
Think back to the Nurenburg trials; did they accept those
same excuses?
I remember the outcome clearly: they ended their days in nooses.

Clive Goldsmith

I'M NORMAL

What's happened to my conscience?
I'm like a little kid
I'm flustered and bewildered
And reviled by what I did

I know it wasn't my fault
But that don't ease the pain
I didn't make it happen
But it happened just the same

I really can't forget it
Or put it to one side
I'd say it never happened
But I think you'll know I've lied

It's too hard to conceal it
The world will know my plight
Then I'll be in trouble
And I'll blush, with shame, tonight

So what's the point in lying?
I'm not a little kid
I shouldn't be bewildered
Or reviled by what I did

I didn't make it happen
I'm really not that smart
I'll just admit I'm normal
And confess, I done a fart.

Ken Mulligan

Springtime

It's Easter time, the season's spring
Creatures awake and birds do sing
Daffodils, crocuses and tulips bloom
The world's awakening out of its gloom.

Jesus from His death did rise
Much to everyone's surprise
He gave us hope, He gave us grace
He made this world a better place.

In the kitchen Mother does bake
She makes a delicious simnel cake
Children jump up and down and beg
Can I have a chocolate Easter egg?

Nicola Edis

Zoo Visit

I went to the zoo today
And what did I see,
A monkey eating nuts
And a chimp drinking tea,
A bear swimming in a pool
Keeping himself nice and cool
In the midday sun.

I went to the zoo today
And what did I see,
An elephant with a long trunk,
Standing by a smelly skunk,
A seal swimming in a pool
Keeping himself nice and cool
In the midday sun.

I went to the zoo today
And what did I see,
Children eating ice cream
And mothers drinking tea,
Me falling in a pool
Which is not really cool,
In the midday sun.

H S Burn

YOUNG AT HEART

Would I like to be young again?
Oh, no thanks - I'll just pass
To live it once is one thing
But twice would be a farce.

All the ups and the downs
And the highs and the lows
All that intensity
And the heartache and woes.

The agony and ecstasy
When you're falling in love
Mood swings from deep despair
Up to cloud nine above.

Every minute lasts a year
Till the next time you meet
Then you're walking on air
With wings on your feet.

By the time you can cope
You've reached middle-age
And you look at the young
Through the eyes of a sage.

Well, I've been there and done that
And got the T-shirt -
Still, if there's anyone out there
Perhaps one more try wouldn't hurt!

Betty Nevell

My Daughter's Hair

After two score years and seven
Looking back across the years
The colour of my daughter's hair
Has brought me near to tears
It seems she's not content
With the colour she has got
So dyes it many colours until
One day she'll have done the lot
Sometimes it has been red, then pink
Other times blonde or blue
And just when I am used to it
It's dyed a different hue
My own hair colour has changed
So I shouldn't have much to say
It was a pretty brunette
But now a paler shade of grey.

Daphne Fryer

My Daughter

Her love is immeasurable, her beauty immense
She shines like the sun up above
From the first day I saw her, that small scrap of life
I was filled with undying love.

She is part of my being, my heart and my soul
She is always by my side
I feel such love when I look at her smile
She fills my heart with pride.

I've watched her grow up from a baby so small
To the woman that she is today
I loved to watch her mop of blonde hair
Blow in the wind when she ran out to play.

And still each day, in wonder I stare
She gives my heart such a lift
This beautiful woman, my baby, my child
God's most precious gift.

Cathy Robertson

SELFLESS LOVE

Enter into - only those who know nothing sure, nor steady
Enter into - all of mine, only when you know there is no space outside
Enter onto my pathway after passing through the gate
that is barred and tricked, yet left agape
Enter after my trail signs, only when seeing the flags and hearing the
trumpet music that plays its tunes to no time, nor tone
Enter up to me when you know the climb
Enter down to my soul with cloth to prevent the clime
set on my footsteps even if you cannot follow
set against my blizzard even if you fear to swallow
set afront of me when all there is to lose
set me onto your road when all have paid my dues
Enter only with me into the unknown
when you know of everything and yet still know of none.

Jessie Bruce

I Remember

I remember long, white, sunlit days, yesterday's summers
With warm, swallow-filled, coppery, cornrake evenings
In the sun-dappled days of my distant youth
Long ago, long ago, when the world was beautiful always.

I remember six weeks of freedom, bliss from educational prison
When, with my friends, I ran through the long, green-brown grass
Of late summer, climbed trees and fished in small, brown streams,
In those white remembered days of yesteryear.

I remember lying on our backs in the long, brown grass
Neath the azure canopy watching white galleons sailing by
Thinking and talking of everything and nothing
With those dear friends of mine, who are mostly dead now.

I remember long, sandy, empty, but now Saxon pebbled beaches
Where we swam, paddled, fished for crabs and chased oyster catchers
Oh how we chattered, laughed and ran all through those long summers
With those dear friends of mine, who are mostly dead now.

Wyn Williams

A Poem For You - Yes, It's True, It's For You

One morning whilst I laid in bed
My love to me this is what she said
If you don't behave
You'll wake up dead

Did you say I'll wake up dead
Wake up dead, that's what she said
That's what she said, I'd heard it said
It had been said, I'd wake up dead

But that doesn't matter
I'm more concerned with this fish and its batter
What fish and its batter
And why doesn't it matter?

It's not the fish that's the matter
The matter's the batter
There's too much batter in the batter
That's what's the matter

I said this is a pain
She said don't mention the rain
Rain, rain, I didn't mention the rain
I didn't mention the rain I said again

It's too wet on the pane
This rain
So this rain is too wet, too wet on the pane
Oh in my head, in my head there's a pain
But I love you all the same.

Gary Rawlings

CLAVA CAIRNS

Released from its glacial blanket and imprisoned floor
Earth yawned and stretched, and replaced the shore
The tide's now ebbed and flowed a distant twenty miles or more
Land-locked, this shingle beach a testimony of yore.
Amidst the trees, *Clava Cairns*; three mounds of bonded pebbles
Bonded pebbles; whoever heard of bonded pebbles?
And there he lay a thousand years and today
Curled up in his sleep with a pot made of clay.
Was he a chief? Or maybe a wise one of his day
In his bonded dome, with radiating lines of lei.

Here I stood in the middle of the day
Autumnal sun, hot, drying the fields of hay
I thought of him, him of no name
A sense of foreboding shook my frame
Thro' this sunlit hollow, an icy breath fell on me
I was an intruder, this was apparent to me.
Uncomfortable I felt, a sense of shame
I left the place and its man of no name
Intrusion of privacy, no respect for the dead
Curiosity about bonded pebbles filled my head
Who? What? Or why was he?
Did not really interest me
All I had was a curiosity
Bonded pebbles stronger than the concrete of today.

Andy Quinn

Amour Courtis

I am a shining knight who has no shield
To keep me safe when called upon to fight.
Rejection is the weapon which you wield
And savage is the blow with which it strikes.

I am a shining knight who has no horse
On which to ride and sweep you off your feet.
Alone it is I must pursue my course
Until my heart's long journey is complete.

I am a shining knight who has no sword
To hold aloft in glorious salute
Then fight with your revered love as reward
And smote down all the rivals to my suit.

Let perseverance then act as my shield
To guard against what wounding words may come
For no slur cuts too deeply to be healed
When at such stout defences it's been slung.

Let patience then become the noble steed
That gallops over all love's rocky ground,
Until the reign of words gives way to deeds
And as the queen of my heart you've been crowned.

Let my devotion be the vaulted blade
I draw to prove my greater worth to you.
With mighty swings I'll cut a crescent swathe
Through suitors who would prove themselves untrue.

For, Lady, I will serve you with what arms
The virtues in my human form create.
Protect you from all those who'd do you harm
And shape our lives into a common fate.

Chris Scriven

Do You Remember?

The air raid shelter was our salvation
Standing at the edge of our reservation
The place where we stood our ground
When bombs were falling all around

I was then only at a very tender age
But I still recall that sudden outrage
The school blitzed one terrible night
Fortunately no children were in sight

The fire station just down the road
A direct hit, a stray bomb did explode
Many died on that very fateful day
Memories forever will never go away

Wardens patrolled, watching over us all
Looking for safety whatever may befall
Hearts beating fast as drones drew nigh
Bombers overhead, some people may die

But the bulldog was waiting at the door
To let unwanted intruders know the score
A new dawn arising, new future in sight
But first invaders had to be put to flight

War broke out in nineteen thirty-nine
Men were called up to join the front line
To defend the country they loved so dear
To die for the kinsfolk they had no fear.

Norman S Brittain

DID YOU SENSE ME COMING?

Did you sense me coming? through the trees
hair in the breeze
on the hill, searching
Did you hear me coming? on the waves
emotion tide sprays
in the sand, sinking footprints
reassuring touch
the promise of so much
Did you sense me coming? my thoughts of you
longings around the fire
flickering, secret shadows
floating smoke
Obsessed
Feelings crowd, diffuse out, emote.

Kelly Swayne

FAREWELL BRIGHTON SEA

The fiery half-moon glowing miles away,
The large, dark sea is pregnant with the secrets of the day.
But, the white waves come leaping to whisper their grey tale
Of the deeply engraved wounds of a missed nightingale.

I can hear the nightingale singing its sweet song
That was lost away among a sour, blind throng.
Everything in the lyric is an epic by itself
To the world to learn to see beyond the self.

I stood in awe in front of the sea to bury
The long hours of gushed flames of fury.
Farewell Brighton sea, farewell my dear friend,
In your bosom will dwell our cherished blend.

Hayat Diyen

SEPTEMBER 11TH

To those who
were sacrificed
we weep for you
if only we knew
what it all
was for
and how we all fell
on that dark day
in this relentless
war against
ourselves.

Steve Gunning

A SPECIAL PLACE

(Inspired by a visit to Alnwick Castle)

Cascades of water
Roses smelling so sweet
Castle made from bricks and mortar
A perfect place to meet
Noble Duchy of Northumberland
Stands majestic on the river Aln
So beautiful, so natural
Was it really built by man?

Joy McFaul

THE FALL

Autumn shades so soft and mellow
Smoky fires and falling leaves
Rich reds and golden yellow
Autumn shades so soft and mellow
If a sound, would be a cello
As gentle notes it does weave
Autumn shades so soft and mellow
Smoky fires and falling leaves.

Suzanne Thorne

THE BRIGHTEST CHRISTMAS DAY

Christmas Day,
Christmas Day,
During Christmas Day we pray
For bright and sunshine days in our life!
We pray for peace and long life of our child, husband and wife!
There is an old wine with a nice label
And a fat turkey hen on our table!
Big Ben sounds unusually!
In this day the Christ was born!
With the faith in heart each man is not alone all along!
The smell of the Christmas tree,
The dream's free!
Sincere spree!
When we hear Jingle Bell
The God's name we gladly spell!
Although the weather is cold and my hand in glove,
I propose a toast to the day of eternal love!

Petr Nicolayevich Maltsev

Sunday School Teachers

What is a teacher? One who shares
what he knows with others.
In the church, we share what God shows us
with our sisters and our brothers.

We all are teachers, by our lives,
and the words we say;
Exemplifying to all we meet
the right, or the wrong way!

But some are called in a more formal way
to teach by word and deed,
every Sunday, week after week,
children's lives they feed.

Classrooms of children, busy and noisy,
Sunday's here again!
How do we interest them, how do we teach them
the word to keep them from sin?

The age of computers, TV and movies
may have changed the way we teach,
but the truth never changes, God never changes!
It's a child's heart He wants to reach.

Some teachers are very creative and gifted,
ideas come easy for them;
others struggle to communicate lessons
the very best way that they can!

Parents are responsible to train in the way,
so their children will follow the Son;
then what should we do, we who are teachers?
Just love them all, one by one!

Mary Alice McAlister

Some Words For Dads

Domestically, the guidelines are sincere,
Going right through the logic, persisting with the proof
Illumines both aspects, the complete penetration,
And also the ordinariness of the concepts . . .
Whilst various clubs spotlight their own goals and
Also the buried crypts of their secrets . . .
Sincerity even from the seemingly outmoded makes homely sense.

M Courtney Soper

EASY TO LEARN ALPHABET

A is for *apple* that keeps the doctor away
B is for *bread* we eat every day
C is for *camera* we all say cheese
D is for *dust* it makes us sneeze
E is for *eagle* that flies in the sky
F is for *fort* that's built up high
G is for *garage* a place for a car
H is for *hill* we climb up so far
I is for *ice* which to touch is cold
J is for *junior*, we're growing old
K is for *kettle* that makes water hot
L is for *lemons,* bitter or what?
M is for *map* that shows us the way
N is for *night* which comes after day
O is for *orang-utan,* a big, furry thing
P is for *piano* around which we all sing
Q is for *queen* the female bee
R is for *rainbow* bright to see
S is for *strawberry* small and sweet
T is for *towel* all folded and neat
U is for *unicorn* that looks like a horse
V is for *violin* we play it of course
W is for *wind* that can blow us away
X is for *X-ray*, we may need one some day
Y is for *yawn* we do when we're tired
Z is for *zoo* where animals are admired.

Nicola Joy Moore

WEDDING

The night before the wedding the bride celebrates.
With drinks at her place, she shares with mates.

While the groom celebrates his last night as a single man.
'Come on mate, just one more can.'

It's lovely to see the bride in her finery of the day.
Groom standing beside her as she holds her bouquet.

Two people so much in love, it's lovely to be.
All their friends and family gathered around to see.

They make a lovely couple as now man and wife.
They have made their vows together for the rest of their life.

We are very proud of them which we cannot hide.
With eyes full of tears, yes we're the parents of the bride.

Barbara Jackson

It's Hard Work Being Handsome

(Dedicated to my Narcissus friend. He knows who he is)

I went out to the nearest seaside,
To see the billowing, noisy waves.
I erred and took my shirt off,
Little did I know the trouble it caused.
It's hard work being handsome.

As I strolled towards the shining sand,
Surrounded by the beautiful local maids,
Panic broke out as I passed slowly by,
They had to call the riot police to save me
It's hard work being handsome.

To return to my car, escorted as I was,
Lassies throwing roses, violets and kisses.
The policeman told me as polite as he could,
For causing the riot, go and don't come back.
It's hard working being handsome.

I wend my way for all to see,
This way, then that, sometimes slowly,
Not too slow, for that would mean,
Riots, young women fighting over me.
It's hard work being handsome.

So one day, the day will come,
My good looks will crumble and go,
perhaps, someone as handsome as me,
Will take up the challenge, but to fail,
It's hard work being handsome.

Jim Livermore

The Teaspoon Famine

There was a terrible teaspoon famine
In the grumpy borough of East Sheen
Alone in a squalid, desolate flat
(You had even taken the pet plague rat)
With aching feet and weeping eyes
I fought my way through love miasma and flies
To attempt to assemble the cup that cheers
But having no teaspoons settled for tinned beers.

Christina Prout

LOVE YOU HAVE INSIDE!

Love is one thousand words,
If you read between the lines,
It gives a warm, caring sound,
If it is said at the right time.

It sometimes causes pain
And is a reason for hatred,
But most of the time makes happiness,
Joy and loving care.

If you make a promise
And swear it on your life,
You will find one day,
The love you have inside.

Becky Moores (11)

My Angel

She wraps her feathered
Wings around me,
Protecting me from all that harms.
She makes me feel so loved and cared for,
Held forever in her arms.

Charlotte E Webb (14)

What's Wrong With Me?

I'm not quite sure what's wrong with me,
but I'm just not feeling right,
I've never felt this way before,
until the other night.
I'm not quite sure what's wrong with me,
the doctor's puzzled too,
he's done so many checks on me,
but hasn't got a clue.
I'm not quite sure what's wrong with me,
I've no rash and I've not been sick,
maybe I'll take a little nap,
that might do the trick.
I'm not quite sure what's wrong with me,
I've really thought it through,
it's only started happening,
since I went out to lunch with you.
I think I know what's wrong with me,
at first I wasn't sure,
but every time I see you,
it happens more and more.
I do, I know what's wrong with me
and I know it must be true,
I don't know how it happened,
but I've fallen in love with you.

Kelly Scurfield

INFORMATION

We hope you have enjoyed reading this book - and that you will continue to enjoy it in the coming years.

If you like reading and writing poetry drop us a line, or give us a call, and we'll send you a free information pack.

Alternatively if you would like to order further copies of this book or any of our other titles, then please give us a call or log onto our website at www.forwardpress.co.uk

Poetry Now Information
Remus House
Coltsfoot Drive
Peterborough
PE2 9JX
(01733) 898101